NTC Language Masters

for Beginning GERMAN Students

Seán Connolly with Clare Cooke

National Textbook Company
a division of *NTC Publishing Group* • Lincolnwood, Illinois USA

Permission is granted to teachers to photocopy the Activity Sheets for classroom use only.

This edition first published 1996 by National Textbook Company,
a division of NTC Publishing Group,
4255 W. Touhy Avenue, Lincolnwood (Chicago), Illinois U.S.A. 60646-1975.
© 1994 Language Centre Publications Ltd.
All Rights Reserved. No part of this book may be reproduced,
stored in a retrieval system, transmitted in any form
or by any means, electronic, mechanical, photocopying, recording, or
otherwise, without the prior permission of NTC Publishing Group.
Printed in the United States of America.

5 6 7 8 9 VP 0 9 8 7 6 5 4 3 2 1

TABLE OF CONTENTS

Teacher's Notes	v
Answer Key	ix
In meiner Schultasche	Sheets 1-6
Ich liebe Tiere!	Sheets 7-13
In der Stadt	Sheets 14-19
Die Sportarten	Sheets 20-25
Mjam mjam!	Sheets 26-31
Betrachte die Farben!	Sheets 32-37
Meine Familie	Sheets 38-43
Bei mir zu Hause	Sheets 44-49

TEACHER'S NOTES

NTC Language Masters for Beginning German Students provides activities on photocopiable worksheets that can be used for students in the early stages of language learning to introduce and reinforce basic vocabulary across a range of topics. Even more advanced students will enjoy the worksheets as they review previously introduced vocabulary.

The topics, which are independent of one another, can be used in any order and adapted for use in any type of teaching/learning context. As far as possible, the activities are self-explanatory and the directions short. Instructions, where they appear, are in the target language. You may want to add extra instructions before copying or explain the sheet verbally where necessary.

Topic Setup

Within each of the eight topics, a similar format has been used, providing a certain amount of progression from the first sheet to the last. Most topics have six activity sheets. Here is the setup and progression for each topic:

1st Sheet:
- Provides a visual presentation of vocabulary that students can use for reference as they work on later sheets.
- Labels can be blocked out before copying to test vocabulary.
- Sheet can be enlarged and colored by students to make posters.

2nd Sheet:
- Generally a game sheet. It can be used for picture/word matching activities, including simple ones in which students write numbers or letters to match words and pictures.
- Sheet can be copied on heavy paper, cut up, and used in various kinds of matching games, such as Concentration-type games or games in which students need to make some kind of association between items.
- Sheet can be copied on heavy paper to make dominoes.
- It can be used for card games such as Fish.
- Sheet can be used for various other speaking activities, picture dictation, stimulus for role play, and question-and-answer activities.

3rd/4th Sheets: Provide a range of activities based on matching pictures and words; often the words are complete, but in some cases, students put together or unscramble words. This helps with reading and recognition, and reinforces spelling. Students could complete the sheets either from memory or by looking at the first sheet for reference.

5th/6th Sheets: The words to be practiced no longer appear on the sheet. Other language often appears on the sheets. The activities require students to complete them from memory (although the first sheet for each topic, with the words, could be referred to at any time by those who need it). The activities rely more on language clues rather than visual clues, but there is still a puzzle element involved.

Suggestions for Use

- Photocopy the first sheet for each topic or the second sheet (*Spielkarte*) onto a transparency for whole class presentation and vocabulary practice.
- Photocopy the first sheet for each topic onto heavy paper (in a different color) so that students can see where to go for help when and if they need it.

- Use for independent work or reinforcement of vocabulary while the class is working on a topic.
- Use for end-of-class or fill-in activities.
- Have students keep a personal record of the sheets they have completed.
- Use sheets for review, homework, or fill-in lessons.

Specific directions for sheets are given below.

IN MEINER SCHULTASCHE

SHEET 3   Although this sheet introduces *mein, meine,* and *meinen,* the students only have to recognize the item of vocabulary and draw it in the appropriate box. They might write out a sentence about each one, e.g., *Mich habe meinen Taschenrechner.*

The grid at the bottom can be used for this and any other topic in the pack. It can be used in a variety of ways: Students can fill in the empty squares with pictures of words from a particular topic. Working in pairs, through question and answer, they then can attempt to discover the items their partner has chosen. For example, STUDENT A: *"B1, Ist das ein Kugelschreiber?"* STUDENT B: *"Nein, das ist kein Kugelschreiber."* If the answer is yes, then A can have a second attempt; if not, it is B's turn. As in the game "Battleships," the winner is the first person who correctly guesses all items and locations. The game can be limited and made easier by providing a list of the items to be used, or by blocking out some of the squares before copying.

SHEET 4   Each sentence gives a clue to a letter; the letters spell out a mystery object. Students may then make up their own *Was bin ich?*

SHEET 5   By spelling out *Taschenrechner,* students can begin to fill in the letters represented by the symbols. From these, they can then go on to figure out what they are being asked to draw for the other coded words. Gradually they can fill in all the letters at the bottom of the sheet.

SHEET 6   Crossword. *Schultasche* is the extra word.

ICH LIEBE TIERE!

SHEET 10   Students mark all the animal names found inside the pictures, or copy out the lists. The word *Schnecke* is introduced with the picture. Students can then fill in their own words and make their own word chain.

SHEET 12   Anagrams on food bowls are to be joined to the correct animal.

SHEET 13   Students complete the notes by adding the names of the pets pictured. They might use the notes as models to write their own.

IN DER STADT

SHEET 16   Starting from the square labeled school (*Schule*), the symbol in that square identifies the place to be moved to next (in this case, to the *Café*). At any time, students can move only to a square that touches the one they are on. Students fill in the places visited on the grid below.

SHEET 17   Students look at the first plan and then the second to see which places have changed. Students then check off these places on the grid. Plans could also be used by students in pair tasks: some items could be blocked out before copying and then used for information gap activities, e.g., *Das Kino ist zwischen.* ... At the bottom, students find one word in each grid.

SHEET 18   Students fill in the missing vowels to complete the sign posts. Students in pairs could then give each other one letter at a time for the other to guess the destination.

SHEET 19   Multiple choice answers to complete the sentences. For the second task, students could complete the sentences and then make up some nonsense possibilities, either using language on the page or adding their own.

DE SPORTARTEN

SHEET 22   Students match the three pictures given to the four words to find the word that doesn't belong. New vocabulary: *Golf, Squash, Federball, Boxen,* and *Karate.* Second activity: Pictures give a clue to the category. Students find the word that doesn't belong.

SHEET 23   Students read the sentence and match it to the sport.

SHEET 25   Students identify the picture extract to name the sport. More advanced students could write a sentence about the sport, giving their opinions, etc.

MJAM MJAM!

SHEET 28   Anagrams for foods in a café. Students complete the bill from the words at the top of the sheet.

SHEET 29   Students figure out picture clues to complete the grid. They can write their results in sentences, e.g., *Es gibt drei Brötchen.*

SHEET 30   Students plan their own party and make up a menu for food and drink.

SHEET 31   A lot of new vocabulary is used here. The activity may only be accessible to more advanced students who have a German dictionary available.

BETRACHTE DIE FARBEN!

SHEET 34   Students follow the arrows through the grid to complete the sentences. From the object, they move to the correct color. The arrow points to the next object. Some explanation of *Pech, was!* and *Hier nicht!* may be needed.

SHEET 35   Students find the color that doesn't belong.

SHEET 36   Anagrams in which the picture is not always a clue to the correct color.

SHEET 37   Introduces *Sonne* as a mystery word. Three new words—*Kreis, Dreieck,* and *Quadrat*—are introduced. Concept of "e" in *Kreise, Dreiecke,* and *Quadrate.* The sheet can be cut in half and this covered in more depth if necessary.

MEINE FAMILIE

SHEET 41   Listing words can be done from memory or from sheet 38. There is no need to add in the names. Students can then write sentences about their own family from these models.

SHEET 42   From words given, students begin to crack the code, and with reference to the names of family members on sheet 38, they can complete the other words and discover the name of the dog.

SHEET 43   Includes words for dog, rabbit, and television. Students might write a letter in reply.

BEI MIR ZU HAUSE

SHEET 46   Students match up two halves of words in the windows, from memory or with sheet 44.

SHEET 47   First activity: Students connect simple sentences to the rooms in the house. Second activity: Students unravel word boxes to find things in the house.

SHEET 48   Students identify mystery objects from the large picture and write which room they come from. More advanced students could then add further information about the room.

SHEET 49   Students could draw the house and add their own information to change some of the details, or write about their own house or a fantasy house.

ANSWERS

IN MEINER SCHULTASCHE

Tätigskeitsblatt 3   Ich habe ... vergessen
(Pictures of) Kugelschreiber, Radiergummi, Buch, Klebstoff, Schultasche, Bleistift, Heft, Filzstifte, Zirkel.

Tätigskeitsblatt 4   Was bin ich?
Filzstift

Tätigskeitsblatt 5   Was is das? - Taschenrechner
Klebstoff, Heft, Spitzer, Zirkel

Tätigskeitsblatt 5   Welcher Buchstabe?
t, a, s, c, h, e, n, r, u, g, k, l, i, p, o, f, z, b.

Tätigskeitsblatt 6   Kreuzworträtsel

Waagerecht	Senkrecht
1. Radiergummi	1. Mäppchen
2. Bleistift	2. Zirkel
3. Lineal	3. Taschenrechner
4. Kugelschreiber	4. Klebstoff
5. Heft	5. Filzstifte

Und was noch? Schultasche.

ICH LIEBE TIERE

Tätigskeitsblatt 10   Suche die Tiere!
(Spider's web) Spinne, Kuh, Katze, Meerschweinchen, Schlange, Schildkröte, Hund, Pferd, Kaninchen, Fisch, Papagei, Schaf.
(Snake) Kaninchen, Katze, Schildkröte, Hund, Pferd, Papagei, Fisch, Kuh, Maus, Schlange.

Tätigskeitsblatt 11   Finde die Wörter!
Fisch, Papagei, Spinne, Kuh, Pferd, Maus, Schaf, Kaninchen, Schlange, Hund.

Tätigskeitsblatt 12   Für wen ist das?
Schlange, Schildkröte, Hund, Fisch, Maus, Papagei, Kaninchen, Pferd, Schwein.

Tätigskeitsblatt 13   Bei mir zu Hause
ein Kaninchen, eine Spinne, Schlange, Katzen, einen Fisch, eine Schildkröte, eine Maus, ein Pferd.

Tätigskeitsblatt 13   Kreuzworträtsel
Waagerecht: Schlange, Katze, Hund, Papagei. *Senkrecht:* Schildkröte, Spinne, Maus.

IN DER STADT

Tätigskeitsblatt 16   Ich gehe nach Hause.
1. Schule 2. Café 3. Kino 4. Kirche 5. Museum 6. Bank 7. Bahnhof 8. Postamt 9. Verkehrsamt 10. Schwimmbad 11. Polizeiwache 12. Sportzentrum 13. Rathaus 14. Supermarkt 15. Parkplatz. 16. Bei mir zu Hause!

Tätigskeitsblatt 17   Stadtpläne
die Schule, das Schwimmbad, das Kino, die Polizeiwache, das Postamt..

Tätigskeitsblatt 17
A. die Schule **B.** das Museum **C.** die Kirche **D.** der Markt

Tätigskeitsblatt 18   Wohin gehst du?
Ki<u>no</u>, <u>P</u>oli<u>zei</u>wa<u>che</u>, <u>Kirche</u>, <u>Sch</u>ule, <u>R</u>at<u>haus</u>, <u>B</u>ahn<u>hof</u>, <u>P</u>ark<u>platz</u>, <u>S</u>port<u>zentrum</u>, <u>M</u>arkt, <u>V</u>er<u>kehrsa</u>mt.
Tätigskeitsblatt 18   Worträtsel
Schwimmbad, Bank, Super(markt), Kirche, (Park)platz, Kino, Café, Postamt, Rathaus, Schule.
Tätigskeitsblatt 19   Ein Quiz
1. zum Markt 2. zum Sportzentrum 3. am Postamt 4. ins Museum 5. am Bahnhof.
Tätigskeitsblatt 19   Ich möchte...ich brauche...
ein Kino, eine Bank, ein Schwimmbad, ein Verkehrsamt, ein Café.

DIE SPORTARTEN

Tätigskeitsblatt 22   Such' den Eindringling!
Tanzen, Jogging, Schwimmen, Golf, Radsport, Tennis.
Reiten, Jogging, Radsport, Skilaufen, Schwimmen.
Tätigskeitsblatt 23   Ein Quiz
1. Tennis 2. Volleyball 3. Segeln 4. Basketball 5. Radsport 6. Skilaufen 7. Tanzen 8. Judo 9. Reiten 10. Schwimmen.
Tätigskeitsblatt 24   Such' die Sportarten!
Segeln, Fußball, Volleyball, Kanufahren, Skilaufen, Jogging, Schwimmen, Tanzen, Basketball, Judo, Tennis.
Tätigskeitsblatt 24   Sieh' die Zeichnungen an!
Golf, Karate, Squash.
Tätigskeitsblatt 25   Welcher Sport ist das?
1. Volleyball 2. Basketball 3. Schwimmen 4. Segeln 5. Judo 6. Skilaufen 7. Kanufahren 8. Jogging 9. Fußball 10. Tennis

MJAM MJAM!

Tätigskeitsblatt 28   Was kostet das?
das Hähnchen, das Brötchen, die Pizza, die Limonade, der Hamburger, die Bohnen, die Chips, die Milch, die Pommes frites, das Eis, die Cola.
Tätigskeitsblatt 28   Die Rechnung
Pommes frites 2 DM, Milch 1,99 DM, Cola 1,85 DM, 2 Hamburgers 10 DM, Chips 70 pf, Eis 1,50 DM SUMME: 18,04 DM.
Tätigskeitsblatt 29   Ich habe...gegessen!
3 Brötchen, 4 Hamburgers, 2 Colas, 3 Hähnchen, 2 Chips, 4 Brote, 3 Eis, 2 Käse, 2 Pizzas, 1 Pommes frites.
Tätigskeitsblatt 30   Die Party
Zum Essen: Erdnüsse, Brot, Chips, Käse, Hamburger, Eis.
Zum Trinken: Cola, Mineralwasser, Limonade, Milch.
Tätigskeitsblatt 31   Wähle A, B oder C!
1. **C** Kartoffeln 2. **A** mit Tomatensoße 3. **B** aus Italien 4. **B** ein Käse 5. **A** Sahne 6. **B** Früchten 7. **A** Früchte und Zucker 8. **C** einem Schwein 9. **A** rot 10. **A** Erdnüsse

BETRACHTE DIE FARBEN!

Tätigskeitsblatt 34   Welche Farbe ist der Luftballon?
1. blau 2. gelb 3. braun 4. grau 5. rosa 6. orange 7. rot 8. grau
Tätigskeitsblatt 35   Such' den Eindringling!
grau, schwarz, blau, violett, rosa, grau

Tätigskeitsblatt 36   Die tollen Farben!
Die seltsamen Schmetterlinge! 1. gelb 2. blau 3. rot 4. grün 5. braun
Welche Farbe ist das? 1. golden 2. grün 3. orange 4. rosa 5. blau
Exotisches Obst 1. orange 2. braun 3. grün 4. violett 5. gelb
Tätigskeitsblatt 37   Welche Farbe bin ich?
Sonne - gelb

MEINE FAMILIE

Tätigskeitsblatt 40   Worträtsel
Bruder, Vetter, Mutter, Vater, Schwester, Großvater, Tante, Sohn, Onkel.
4 Brüder, 3 Schwestern
Tätigskeitsblatt 41   Ergänze die Kasten!
Die Eltern: 1. der Vater 2. die Mutter
Die Großeltern: 1. der Großvater 2. die Großmutter
Die Familie: 1. der Stiefbruder 2. der Bruder 4. ich 4. die Schwester
Brigittes Familie: 1. der Onkel 2. die Tante 3. der Vetter 4. die Kusine
Tätigskeitsblatt 41   Wer ist das?
1. Georg ist mein Großvater. 2. Erika ist meine Kusine. 3. Gerhard ist mein Onkel. 4. Monika ist meine Mutter. 5. Hans ist mein Stiefbruder. 6. Ulrike ist meine Schwester.
Tätigskeitsblatt 42   Hier ist meine Familie
1. der Bruder 2. die Mutter 3. die Tante 4. der Vater 5. der Stiefbruder 6. der Großvater 7. die Kusine 8. die Schwester 9. der Onkel 10. die Stiefmutter
Der Hund heißt FLITTER
Tätigskeitsblatt 42   Welcher Buchstabe ist das?
i, b, l, e, o, m, r, s, u, c, n, a, g, d, p, t, f, k, v, h, w.
Tätigskeitsblatt 43   Ein Brief
Familie, Familie, Bruder, Schwester, Vater, Mutter, Großvater, Hund, Kaninchen, Fernsehen.

BEI MIR ZU HAUSE

Tätigskeitsblatt 46   Wo ist das?
Schlafzimmer, Eßzimmer, Küche, Dachgeschoß, Wohnzimmer, Treppe, Keller, Haus.
Tätigskeitsblatt 47   Wo im Haus?
1 im Wohnzimmer 2. im Eßzimmer 3. im Schlafzimmer 4. im Keller 6. in der Küche 6. im Badezimmer 7. auf der Treppe 8. im Garten
Tätigskeitsblatt 47   Wo ist das?
A. Küche, Keller, Eßzimmer. **B.** Garten, Haus, Treppe. **C.** Küche, Dachgeschoß
Tätigskeitsblatt 48   Welches Zimmer ist das?
1. Das ist das Schlafzimmer. 2. Das ist das Wohnzimmer. 3. Das ist das Eßzimmer. 4. Das ist die Küche. 5. Das ist das Badezimmer. 6. Das ist das Fenster. 7. Das ist die Treppe. 8. Das ist der Keller. 9. Das ist die Haustür. 10. Das ist der Garten.
Tätigskeitsblatt 49   Ein Brief
Haus, Garten, Haustür, ein Wohnzimmer, ein Eßzimmer, Küche, Fenster, Treppe, Schlafzimmer, Badezimmer, Dachgeschoß, Mäuse, ein Keller, Wein.

Tätigskeitsblatt 1

NAME _____

IN MEINER SCHULTASCHE

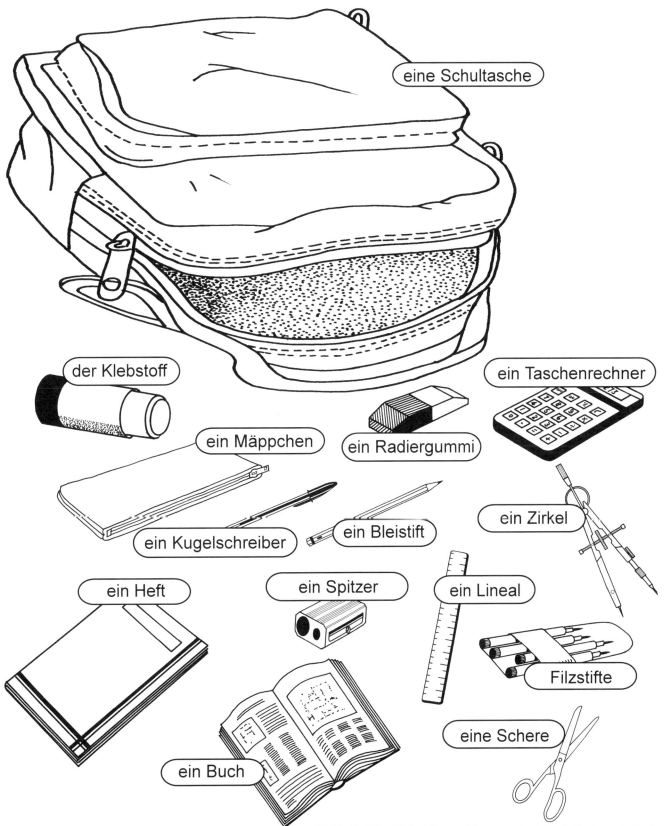

| Tätigkeitsblatt **2** | NAME_____ |

SPIELKARTE

ein Mäppchen 	eine Schultasche 
ein Heft 	ein Bleistift 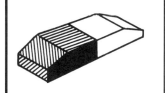
ein Buch 	ein Radiergummi 
ein Lineal 	ein Taschenrechner 
ein Spitzer 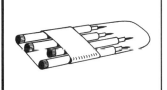	Filzstifte 
ein Zirkel 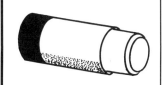	eine Schere 
der Klebstoff 	ein Kugelschreiber 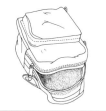

| Tätigkeitsblatt | 3 | | NAME_____ |

ICH HABE .....VERGESSEN

	ruler	calculator	
meinen Kugelschreiber	mein Lineal	meinen Taschenrechner	meinen Radiergummi
	sharpener		
mein Buch	meinen Spitzer	meinen Klebstoff	meine Schultasche
meinen Bleistift	mein Heft	meine Filzstifte	mein Zirkel

	A	B	C	D
1	▓			▓
2		▓		
3		▓		▓

Published by National Textbook Company. This page may be photocopied for classroom use only.

Tätigskeitsblatt 4

NAME_____

WAS BIN ICH?

Mein erster ist in Klebstoff und in Bleistift.

Mein zweiter ist in Radiergummi und in Lineal.

Mein dritter ist in Zirkel und in Kugelschreiber.

Mein vierter ist in Spitzer und in Zirkel.

Mein fünfter ist in Schultasche und in Schere.

Mein sechster ist in Taschenrechner und in Heft.

Mein siebter ist in Lineal und in Bleistift.

Mein achter ist in Heft und in Klebstoff.

Mein neunter ist in Bleistift und in Taschenrechner.

Schere und Schultasche enden mit meinem zehnten.

Und jetzt geh 'weiter!

Schreibe deinen eigenen "Wer bin ich?"

Suche in deiner Schultasche!

Schreibe eine Liste von Sachen, die du da siehst!

Tätigkeitsblatt 5

NAME_____

WAS IST DAS?

Zeichne ....

KUGELSCHREIBER

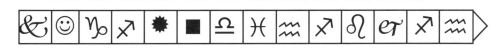 

 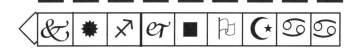

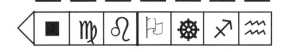

Welcher Buchstabe?

							R										

Tätigskeitsblatt 6

NAME _____

KREUZWORTRÄTZEL

Waagerecht

1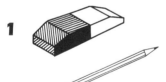

2

3

4

5

Senkrecht

1

2

3

4

5

Und was noch?

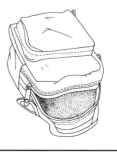

Tätigkeitsblatt 7

NAME _____

ICH LIEBE TIERE!

- eine Katze
- eine Schlange
- eine Spinne
- eine Maus
- ein Papagei
- ein Hund
- ein Meerschweinchen
- ein Fisch
- ein Kaninchen
- eine Schildkröte

Tätigkeitsblatt **9**

NAME _____

SPIELKARTE

ein Schaf		ein Fisch	
eine Katze		eine Kuh	
ein Pferd		ein Schwein	
eine Schildkröte		ein Hund	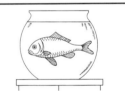
eine Spinne		ein Meerschwein-chen	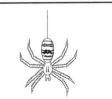
eine Maus		ein Kaninchen	
ein Papagei		eine Schlange	

Published by National Textbook Company. This page may be photocopied for classroom use only.

Tätigkeitsblatt **10**

NAME _____

SUCH' DIE TIERE!

Jetzt bist du dran!
Schreibe die Tiere
in die Schnecke!

Tätigkeitsblatt 11

NAME _____

FINDE DIE WÖRTER!

S	O	U	F	I	S	C	H	O	M
P	A	P	A	G	E	I	E	T	N
E	P	R	H	E	G	C	T	O	E
E	A	U	C	N	N	H	A	R	H
C	N	E	S	R	A	E	H	T	C
D	A	N	N	S	L	V	C	U	N
C	V	H	I	H	H	U	K	E	I
D	R	E	F	P	C	L	T	O	N
O	S	M	A	U	S	S	U	M	A
N	A	T	O	G	R	A	C	S	K

Tätigkeitsblatt 12

NAME _____

FÜR WEN IST DAS?

- gaeshlcn
- tkhclöedsir
- nhdu
- hfcis
- uasm
- eagpiap
- iheck nnan
- rfdep
- wsnihec

Tätigkeitsblatt 13

NAME _____

BEI MIR ZU HAUSE

Liebe Freundin!
Mein Name ist Bärbel und zu Hause habe ich _____.

Hallo Steven! Mein Name ist Franz und ich habe _____.

Lieber Freund!
Ich heiße Markus, Ich habe eine _____.

Hallo Gary! Ich heiße Eva. Ich liebe Tiere und Ich habe zwei _____.

Lieber John!
Mein Name ist Josef und ich habe _____.

Hallo Katy!
Mein Name ist Gabi, und ich habe _____ und _____.

Kreuzworträtsel

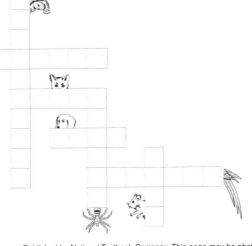

Tätigkeitsblatt 14

NAME _____

IN DER STADT

- das Verkehrsamt
- das Rathaus
- die Kirche
- die Bank
- das Café
- das Museum
- der Parkplatz
- das Kino
- der Supermarkt
- das Postamt
- die Polizeiwache
- der Park
- das Schwimmbad
- der Markt
- die Schule
- der Bahnhof
- das Sportzentrum

Published by National Textbook Company. This page may be photocopied for classroom use only.

Tätigkeitsblatt 15

NAME _____

SPIELKARTE

	der Supermarkt		die Schule
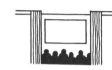	das Schwimmbad		das Café
	der Bahnhof		das Rathaus
	das Postamt		das Verkehrsamt
	die Kirche		das Museum
	das Kino		die Polizeiwache
	die Bank		das Sportzentrum
	der Parkplatz		der Markt

Published by National Textbook Company. This page may be photocopied for classroom use only.

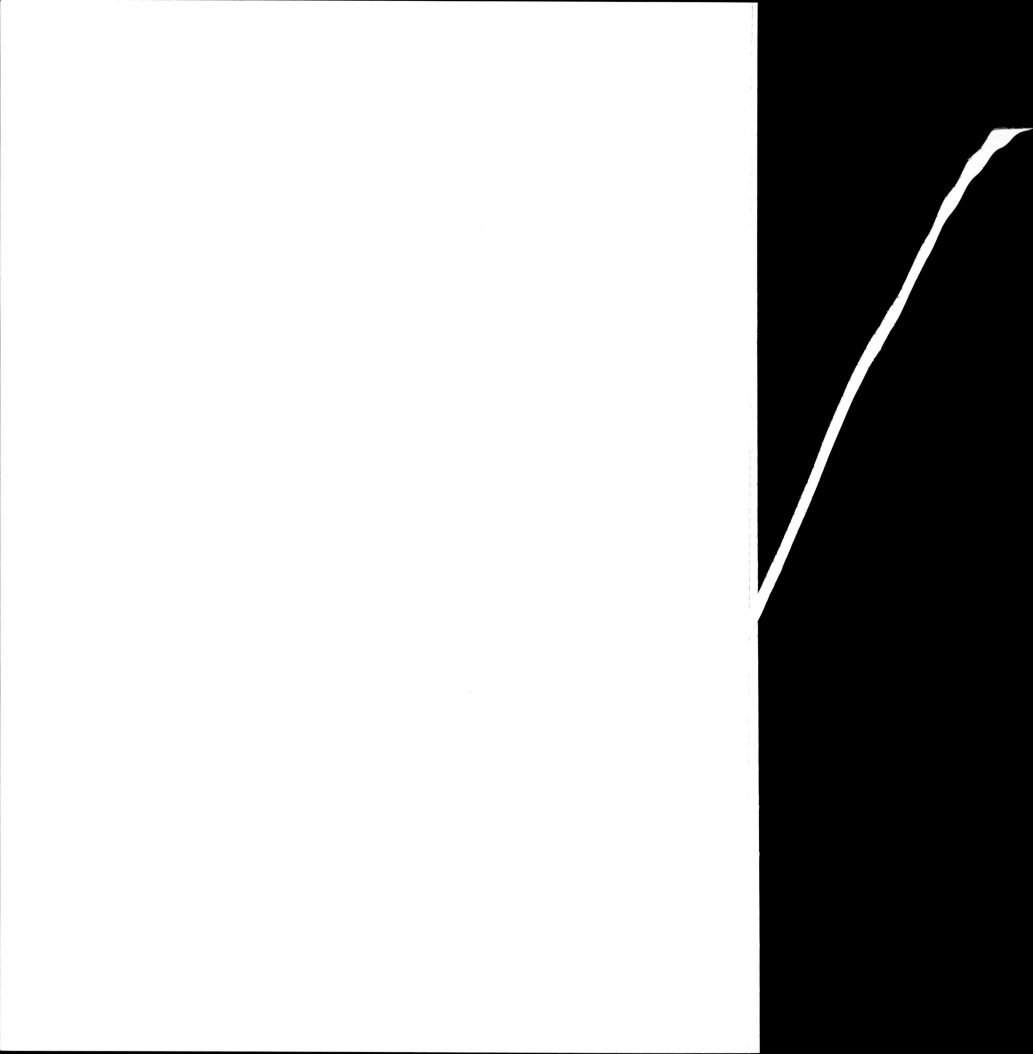

Tätigskeitsblatt 16

NAME _____

ICH GEHE NACH HAUSE.

Fang' an der Schule an!	Park →	Café →	Verkehrsamt →	Verirrt?
Postamt →	Schule →	Schwimmbad →	Kino →	Postamt →
Bahnhof →	Polizeiwache →	Kirche →	Museum →	Bahnhof →
Sportzentrum →	Bank →	Supermarkt →	Park →	Bank →
Museum →	Rathaus →	Schwimmbad →	Parkplatz →	BEI MIR ZU HAUSE!

Wohin gehst du, um nach Hause anzukommen?

1	2	3	4
5	6	7	8
9	10	11	12
13	14	15	16

Tätigskeitsblatt 17

NAME _____

STADTPLÄNE

Guck' mal hier ....

Guck' mal hier!

_ _ _ _ _ _ _ hat geändert ✓

... und dann hier!

die Bank	
der Markt	
das Postamt	
das Café	
die Polizeiwache	
das Kino	
das Verkehrsamt	
das Schwimmbad	
das Museum	
die Schule	

A.

C	H	U
S	D	L
E	I	E

B.

E	S	D
U	U	A
M	M	S

C.

E	I	D
K	I	R
E	H	C

D.

A	M	R
R	✱	E
K	T	D

Published by National Textbook Company. This page may be photocopied for classroom use only.

Tätigskeitsblatt 18

NAME _____

WOHIN GEHST DU?

- _ a _ nh _ _
- K _ _ o
- P _ _ kp _ _ _ z
- _ ol _ _ e _ w _ _ _ e
- S _ _ r _ z _ n _ _ u _
- _ _ rc _
- M _ _ k _
- _ _ hu _ e
- _ erk _ _ r _ a _ t
- _ _ t _ au _

Worträtzel

R	A	I	R	A	S	S	I	M	M	O	K
D	A	N	G	D	O	N	C	U	C	L	I
A	U	T	M	A	T	S	O	P	E	E	N
B	G	P	H	A	L	L	E	A	N	N	O
M	R	I	E	A	L	K	I	R	C	H	E
M	A	S	F	R	U	V	A	K	R	C	G
I	N	B	B	Z	M	S	D	P	Y	S	E
W	E	F	A	C	E	C	M	L	N	I	C
H	A	N	E	N	E	H	R	A	T	P	X
C	S	E	T	S	K	U	O	T	A	F	E
S	S	U	O	T	I	L	E	Z	H	O	R
T	K	R	A	M	R	E	P	U	S	E	O

Finde die zehn verstecken Wörter!

Schreibe die Liste!

_____
_____
_____
_____
_____
_____
_____
_____
_____
_____

Tätigkeitsblatt 19

NAME _____

IN DER STADT : EIN QUIZ

1. Ich möchte einkaufen gehen, ich gehe
   a) zum Schwimmbad.
   b) zum Markt.
   c) zum Museum.

2. Um Basketball zu spielen, gehe ich
   a) zum Supermarkt.
   b) zum Café.
   c) zum Sportzentrum.

3. Ich kaufe eine Briefmarke
   a) in der Kirche.
   b) in der Polizeiwache.
   c) am Postamt.

4. Die Geschichte gefällt mir, also gehe ich oft
   a) ins Museum.
   b) auf die Bank.
   c) ins Hotel.

5. Ich fahre mit dem Zug, also bin ich
   a) am Schwimmbad.
   b) am Bahnhof.
   c) am Museum.

ICH MÖCHTE ...

einen Film ansehen.
Geld wechseln.
schwimmen gehen.
eine Auskunft bekommen.
etwas essen und trinken.

ICH BRAUCHE ...

ein Schwimmbad.
ein Kino.
eine Bank.
ein Café.
ein Verkehrsamt.

Tätigkeitsblatt 21

NAME _____

SPIELKARTE

Fußball		Tanzen	
Volleyball		Tennis	
Basketball		Reiten	
Segeln		Schwimmen	
Radsport		Jogging	
Turnen		Judo	
Skilaufen		Kanufahren	

| Tätigkeitsblatt 22 | NAME _____ |

SUCH' DEN EINDRINGLING!

 Segeln · Fußball · Skilaufen · Tanzen

 Tennis · Jogging · Judo · Kanufahren

 Radsport · Basketball · Volleyball · Schwimmen

  Tanzen · Segeln · Schwimmen · Golf

  Fußball · Judo · Radsport · Jogging

  Tanzen · Tennis · Volleyball · Skilaufen

 Fußball · Volleyball · Golf · Reiten

 Kanufahren · Segeln · Schwimmen · Jogging

 Squash · Tennis · Radsport · Federball

 Rugby · Fußball · Skilaufen · Basketball

 Judo · Boxen · Karate · Schwimmen

Tätigkeitsblatt 23

NAME _____

EIN QUIZ

1. Jeden Sommer findet eine große Meisterschaft in Wimbledon statt.
2. Man spielt das oft am Strand.
3. Für diesen Sport muß es windig sein!
4. Dieser Sport ist für große Spieler.
5. Der Nationalsport Frankreichs.
6. Man geht ins Gebirge für diesen Sport.
7. Dies ist für junge und alte Leute, die Musik lieben.
8. Sehr beliebt in Deutschland und Japan.
9. Für diesen Sport muß man Tiere lieben!
10. Dieser Sport findet in Schwimmbad statt.

Tennis   Radsport
Segeln   Basketball
Schwimmen   Judo
Volleyball   Tanzen
Reiten   Skilaufen

Tätigskeitsblatt **24**

NAME _____

SUCH' DIE SPORTARTEN!

E	N	E	M	M	I	W	H	C	S
N	B	V	R	O	S	S	W	X	O
E	A	O	D	U	J	I	C	O	N
R	S	L	U	V	O	N	U	R	E
H	K	L	A	N	G	N	T	Y	F
A	E	E	S	E	G	E	L	N	U
F	T	Y	B	A	I	T	I	L	A
U	B	B	T	A	N	Z	E	N	L
N	A	A	D	U	G	A	N	O	I
A	L	L	A	B	ß	U	F	V	K
K	L	L	J	R	S	P	T	U	S

Sieh' die Zeichnungen an!

... und noch drei andere? _____ _____ _____

Tätigkeitsblatt 25

NAME _____

WELCHER SPORT IST DAS?

1 _____ 2 _____ 3 _____ 4 _____ 5 _____

6 _____ 7 _____ 8 _____ 9 _____ 10 _____

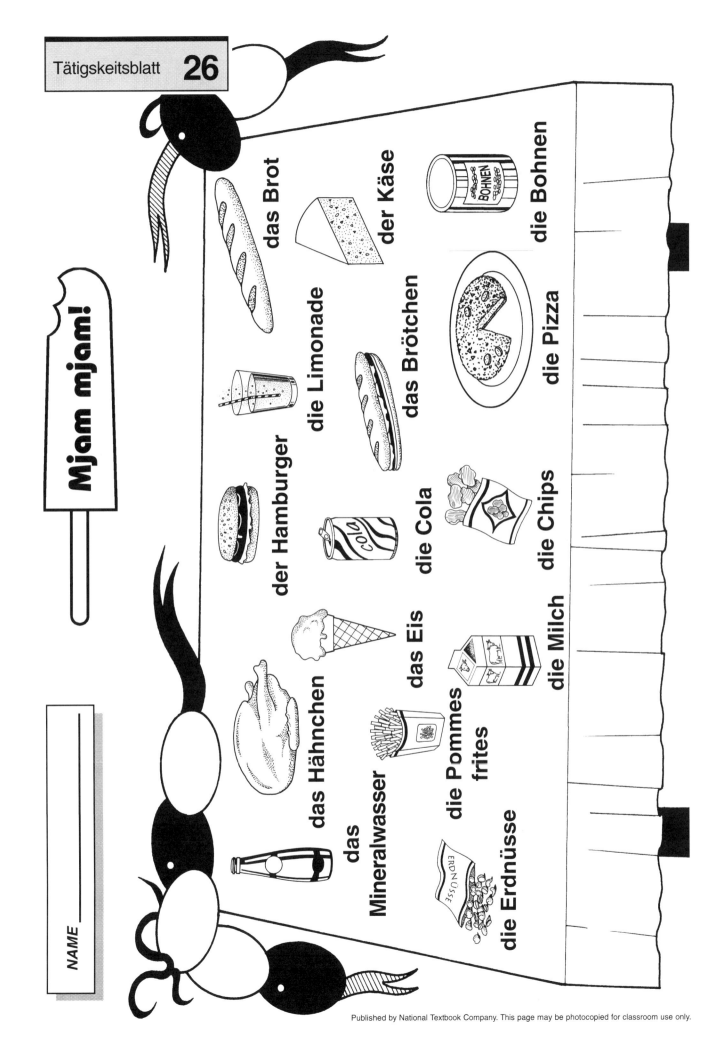

Tätigkeitsblatt 27

NAME _____

Spielkarte

der Chips		der Hamburger	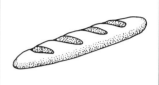
das Mineralwasser		die Bohnen	
der Käse	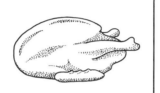	die Cola	
die Milch		die Erdnüsse	
die Pommes frites		das Brot	
das Brötchen	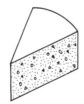	das Eis	
das Hähnchen		die Limonade	

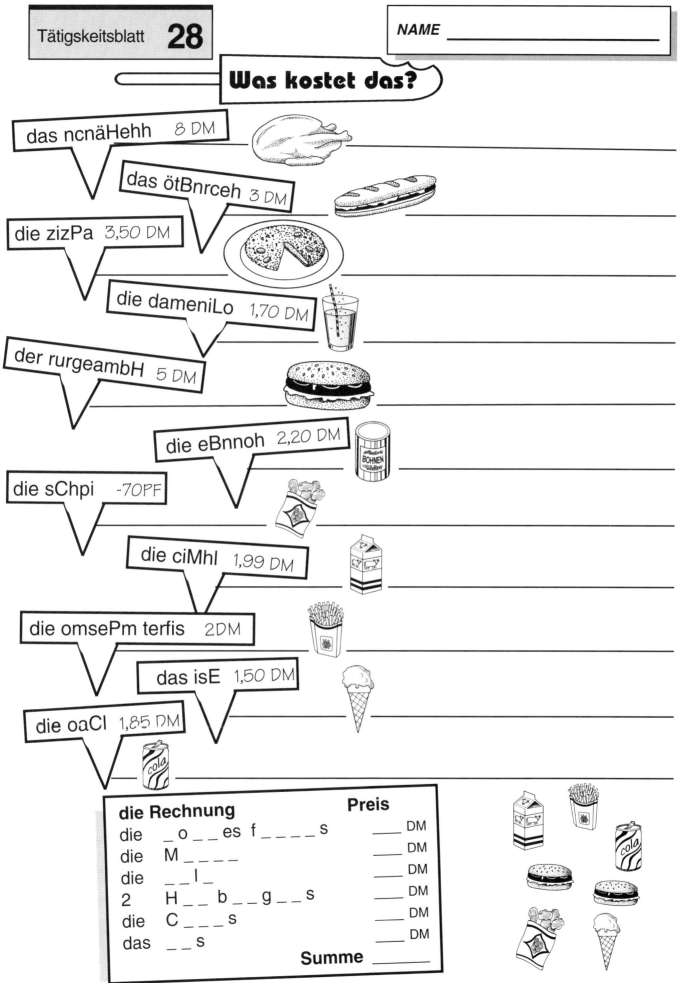

Tätigkeitsblatt 29

NAME _____

Ich habe .... gegessen!

Wieviele hast du gefunden?

3	Brötchen		Brote
	Hamburgers		Eis
	Colas		Käse
	Hähnchen		Pizzas
	Chips		Pommes frites

Tätigkeitsblatt **30**

NAME _____

Die Party

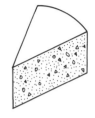

Zum Essen

_____
_____
_____
_____
_____
_____

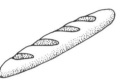
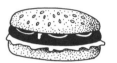

Zum Trinken

_____
_____
_____
_____

Published by National Textbook Company. This page may be photocopied for classroom use only.

Tätigskeitsblatt 31

NAME _____

Wähle a, b, oder c!

1. Man macht Chips aus ....
   - A Äpfel.
   - B Kohl.
   - C Kartoffeln.

2. Die Engländer essen Bohnen ....
   - A mit Tomatensoße.
   - B als Nachtisch.
   - C in ihrem Tee.

3. Pizzas Kommen ....
   - A aus Irland.
   - B aus Italien.
   - C aus Spanien.

4. Limburger ist ....
   - A eine Frucht.
   - B ein Käse.
   - C ein Getränk.

5. Man macht Eis aus ....
   - A Sahne.
   - B Orangensaft.
   - C Zwiebeln.

6. Erdbeeren sind ....
   - A Bohnen.
   - B Früchten.
   - C Insekten.

7. Man macht Marmelade ....
   - A Früchten und Zucker.
   - B Früchten und Sahne.
   - C Früchten und Cola.

8. Schinken kommt von ....
   - A einem Schaf.
   - B einer Kuh.
   - C einem Schwein.

9. Himbeeren sind ....
   - A rot.
   - B grün.
   - C blau.

10. Vegetarier essen ....
    - A Erdnüsse.
    - B Bratwurst.
    - C Schinken.

Tätigkeitsblatt 32

NAME _____

Betrachte die Farben!

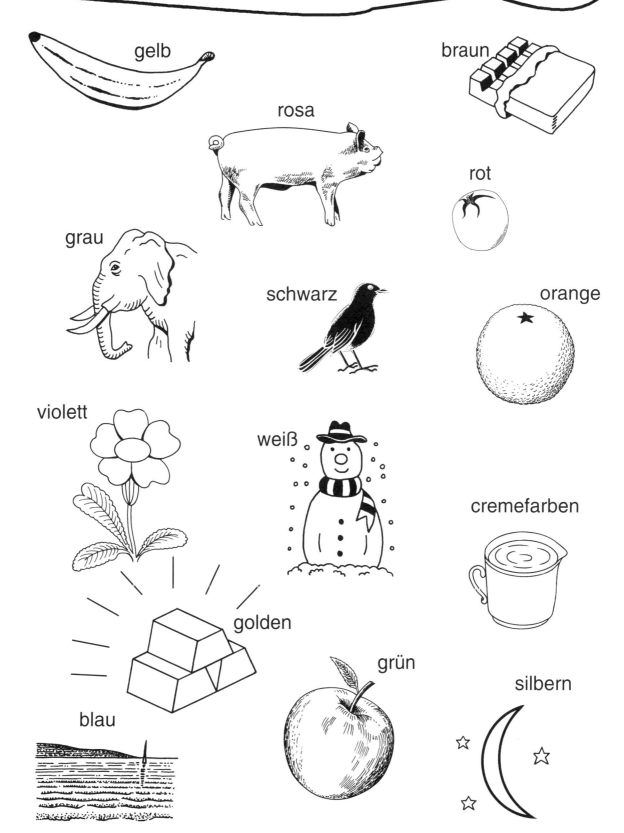

Tätigkeitsblatt 33

NAME _____

Spielkarte

blau		rot	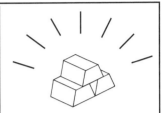
grün		orange	
grau		braun	
schwarz		gelb	
violett		rosa	
weiß		golden	
silbern		cremefarben	

Tätigkeitsblatt **34**

NAME _____

Welche Farbe ist der Luftballon?

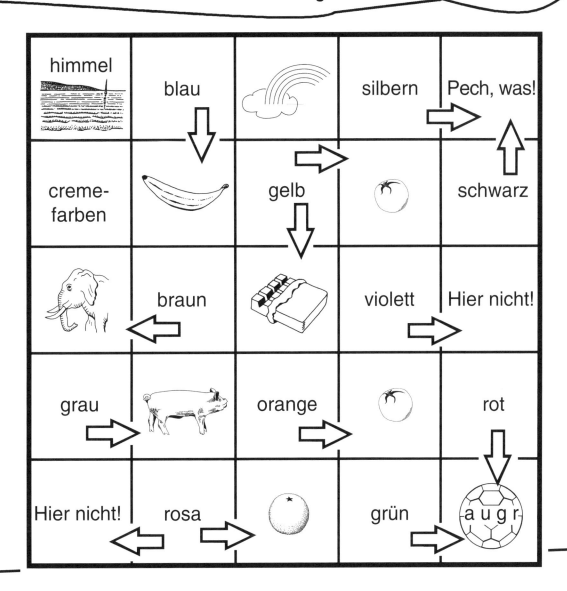

Ergänze die Sätze!

1. Der Himmel ist _____.
2. Die Banane ist _____.
3. Die Schokolade ist _____.
4. Der Elefant ist _____.
5. Der Schwein ist _____.
6. Die Orange ist _____.
7. Die Tomate ist _____.
8. Der Luftballon ist _____.

Tätigkeitsblatt 35

NAME _____

Such' den Eindringling!

   (blau)   grün
         rot   gelb

   orange   grau
         silbern weiß

   braun   rosa
         violett schwarz

   schwarz   rot   gelb   (grün)

   rot   blau   orange   grün

   blau   braun   violett   grün

   rosa   schwarz   braun   weiß

   blau   grün   grau   gelb

Färbe den Regenbogen!

rosa rot orange gelb grün blau violett

KLASSE!

Tätigkeitsblatt 36

NAME _____

Die tollen Farben!

Die seltsamen Schmetterlinge!   Finden die 5 Farben!

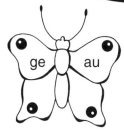  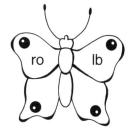 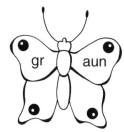 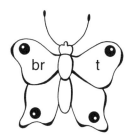

ge au   bl ün   ro lb   gr aun   br t

1. _____ 2. _____ 3. _____ 4. _____ 5. _____

Welche Farbe ist das?

      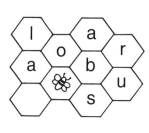

1. _____

2. _____

3. _____

4. _____

5. _____

Exotisches Obst

 = _____

 = _____

 = _____

 = _____

 = _____

Tätigkeitsblatt **37**

NAME _____

Welche Farbe bin ich?

Mein erster ist in rosa und in silbern.

Mein zweiter ist in orange und in rot.

Mein dritter ist in grün aber nicht in grau.

Mein vierter ist in braun und in golden.

Mein fünfter ist in gelb und in orange.

_ _ _ _ _

Zeichne mich und dann färbe! ➡

Ich bin? _ _ _ _

Färbe und schreibe' Sätze!

Kreis   Dreieck   Quadrat

2 Dreiecke sind schwarz.

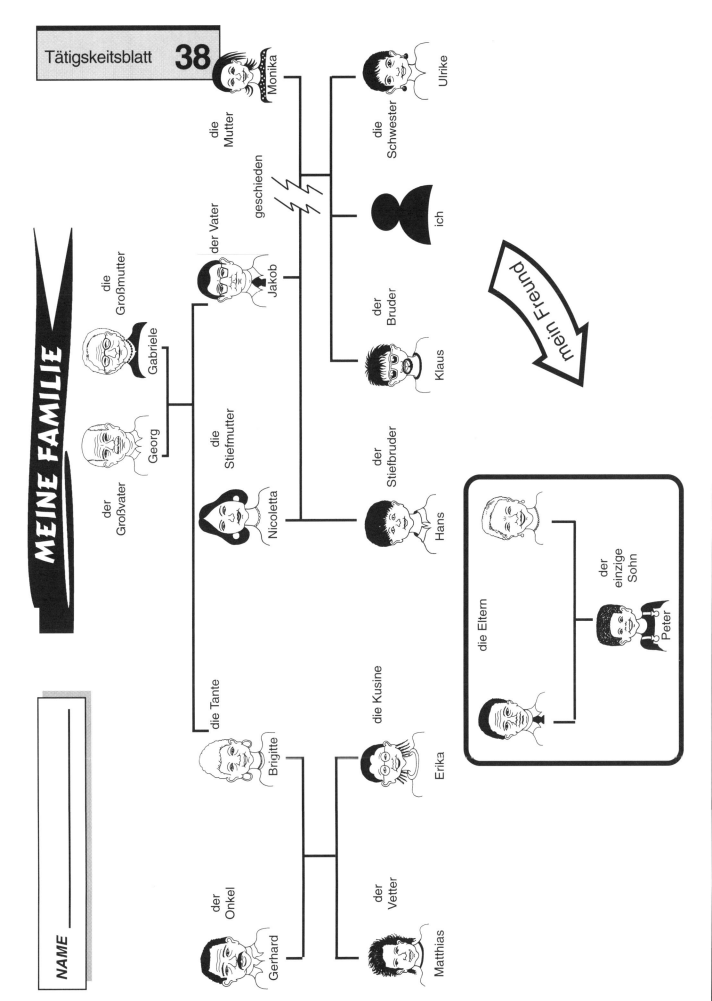

Tätigskeitsblatt **39**

NAME _____

SPIELKARTE

der einzige Sohn	 Jakob	**die Kusine**	Gerhard
der Vater	 Monika	**der Onkel**	Brigitte
die Mutter	 Ulrike	**die Tante**	Gabriele
die Schwester	 Klaus	**die Großmutter**	Georg
der Bruder	 Hans	**der Großvater**	Nicoletta
der Stiefbruder	 Matthias	**die Stiefmutter**	
der Vetter	 Erika	**die Eltern**	 Peter

Published by National Textbook Company. This page may be photocopied for classroom use only.

Tätigkeitsblatt 40

NAME _____

WORTRÄTSEL

Suche die Familie!

E	R	L	A	B	R	U	D	E	R
K	V	E	T	T	E	R	R	E	E
R	M	U	T	T	E	R	T	L	T
E	R	V	I	S	R	S	U	E	S
T	E	E	E	J	E	P	S	K	E
A	T	M	D	W	D	W	A	N	W
V	A	D	H	U	U	X	H	O	H
ß	V	C	B	C	R	O	Y	C	C
O	S	O	H	N	B	B	H	S	S
R	U	F	T	G	E	T	N	A	T
G	W	N	R	E	D	U	R	B	Z

Wieviele Geschwister hast du gefunden?

Published by National Textbook Company. This page may be photocopied for classroom use only.

Tätigkeitsblatt 41

NAME _____

ERGÄNZE DIE KASTEN!

Die Eltern
1. Der Vater
2.

Die Großeltern
1.
2.

Die Familie
1.
2.
3.
4.

Brigittes Familie
1.
2.
3.
4.

Wer ist das?

1. _____ ist meine Tante / mein Großvater / meine Mutter / mein Bruder.

2. _____ ist meine Kusine / mein Vetter.

3. _____ ist mein Vater / mein Großvater / mein Onkel.

4. _____ ist meine Großmutter / meine Tochter / meine Mutter.

5. _____ ist mein Stiefbruder / mein Vater / meine Schwester.

6. _____ ist mein Bruder / meine Stiefmutter / meine Schwester.

Tätigkeitsblatt 42

NAME _____

HIER IST MEINE FAMILIE

Um dir zu helfen ... die Familie = ♓ ♌ ♐ | ♋ ♦ & ♌ ☀ ♌ ♐

D I E F A M I L I E

1. Klaus ist ♓♐♒ | et ♒☺♓♐♒ ___ _____

2. Monika ist ♓♌♐ | &☺♘♘♐♒ ___ _____

3. Brigitte ist ♓♌♐ | ♘♦⧗♘♐ ___ _____

4. Jakob ist ♓♐♒ | ☾♦♘♐♒ ___ _____

5. Hans ist ♓♐♒ | ■♘♌♐♋et♒☺♓♐♒ ___ _____

6. Georg ist ♓♐♒ | ♑♒☪⌘☾♦♘♐♒ ___ _____

7. Erika ist ♓♌♐ | ▲☺■♌⧗♐ ___ _____

8. Ulrike ist ♓♌♐ | ■♎○❖♐■♘♐♒ ___ _____

9. Gerhard ist ♓♐♒ | ☪⧗▲♐☀ ___ _____

10. Nicoletta ist ♓♌♐ | ■♘♌♐♋&☺♘♐♒ ___ _____

Und der Hund, wie heißt er? ♋☀♌♘♘♐♒ _____ !

Welcher Buchstabe ist das?

♌	et	☀	♐	☪	&	♒	■	☺	♎	⧗	♦	♑	♓	♍	♘	♋	▲	☾	○	❖	⌘
			R																		

EIN BRIEF

Hallo Karen!

Mein Name ist Klaus. Ich bin 12 und wohne in Frankfurt. Hier ist ein Foto von meiner .

Wir sind sechs Personen in unserer .

Ich habe einen und eine . Mein heißt Jakob.

Er ist groß. Meine heißt Monika.

Meine Großeltern wohnen auch bei uns.

Mein und meine sind sehr nett!

Ich habe einen und ein .

Ich liebe Tiere und das auch!

Und du, wieviele Personen sind in deiner Familie?

Schreib' mir einen Brief!

Tschüß,

Klaus

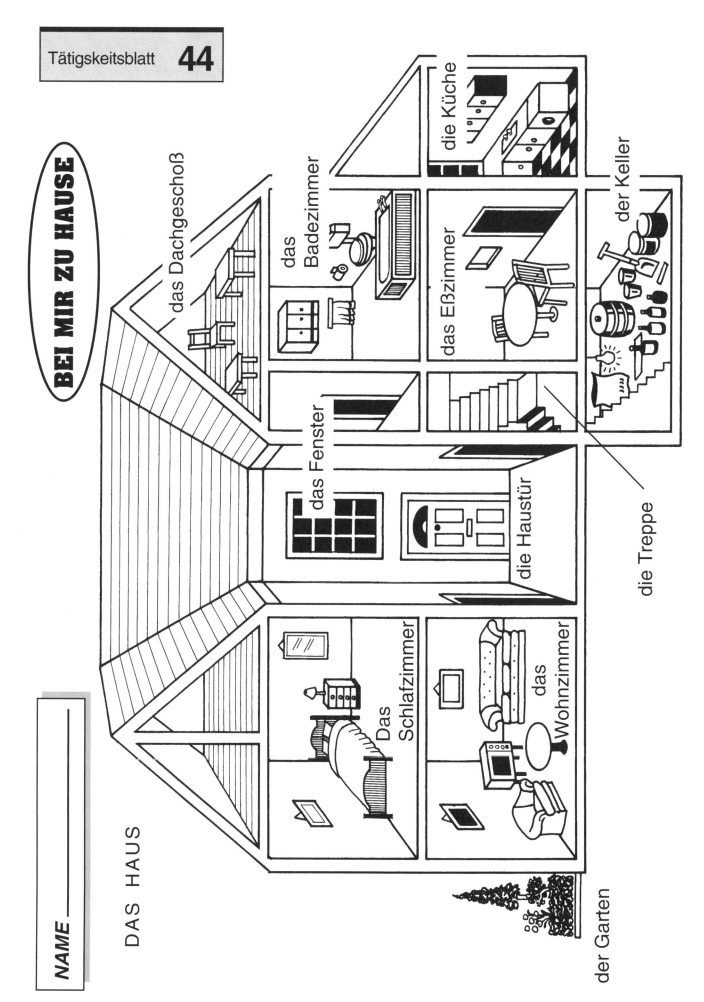

Tätigskeitsblatt **45**

NAME _____

SPIELKARTE

der Keller		**der Garten**	
das Schlafzimmer		**das Wohnzimmer**	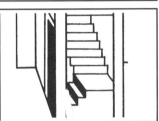
das Eßzimmer	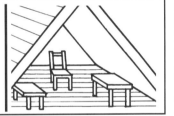	**die Treppe**	
das Dachgesschoß		**das Haus**	
die Haustür		**die Küche**	
das Fenster		**das Badezimmer**	

Published by National Textbook Company. This page may be photocopied for classroom use only.

Tätigkeitsblatt 46

NAME _____

WO IST DAS?

Schlafz	nzimmer
Eßzi	us
Kü	ler
Dachge	immer
Woh	ppe
Tre	che
Kel	schoß
Ha	mmer

Tätigkeitsblatt 47

NAME _____

WO IM HAUS?

Ich bin ...

.. im Schlafzimmer.

.. im Garten.

.. im Eßzimmer.

.. in der Küche.

.. im Keller.

.. im Badezimmer.

.. im Wohnzimmer.

.. auf der Treppe.

1. Ich sehe fern.
2. Ich frühstücke.
3. Ich schlafe.
4. Ich suche einen guten Wein.
5. Ich bereite eine Mahlzeit vor.
6. Ich dusche.
7. Ich gehe zum ersten Stock.
8. Ich schaue die Blumen an.

Wo ist das?

K	Ü	C	H
E	L	L	E
E	R	E	ß
M	M	I	Z

R	A	G	H
T	E	N	A
P	E	S	U
P	E	R	T

S	C	H	C
E	H	E	Ü
G	O	ß	K
H	C	A	D

1. _____
2. _____
3. _____

1. _____
2. _____
3. _____

1. _____
2. _____

Tätigkeitsblatt 48

NAME _____

WELCHES ZIMMER IST DAS?

Kannst du das richtige Zimmer finden?

1 *Das ist das Schlafzimmer.* ✓
2 _____
3 _____
4 _____
5 _____

6 _____
7 _____
8 _____
9 _____
10 _____

Published by National Textbook Company. This page may be photocopied for classroom use only.

EIN BRIEF

Hallo Peter!

Endlich sind wir umgezogen! Das neue  ist echt gut.

Es gibt einen großen und die ist rot!

Im Erdgeschoß gibt es  und .

Es gibt auch eine große .

Im Flur gibt es ein über der .

Im ersten Stock gibt es drei  und ein ,

aber im  gibt es   !!

Wir haben auch  für den .

Du mußt dieses Haus sehen, aber ich habe noch keine Fotos!

Tschüß,

Monika

Zeiche einen Grundriß des Hauses!

NOTES

M.E. BRYAN MIDDLE SCHOOL
605 Independence Road
St. Charles, MO 63304

NOTES